ROOM LAYOUT KIT

1 SQUARE = 1 SQUARE FOOT
SIMPLY DRAW YOUR ROOM SHAPE
ON THE GRAPH PAPER, THEN CUT OUT
AND POSITION THE FURNITURE!

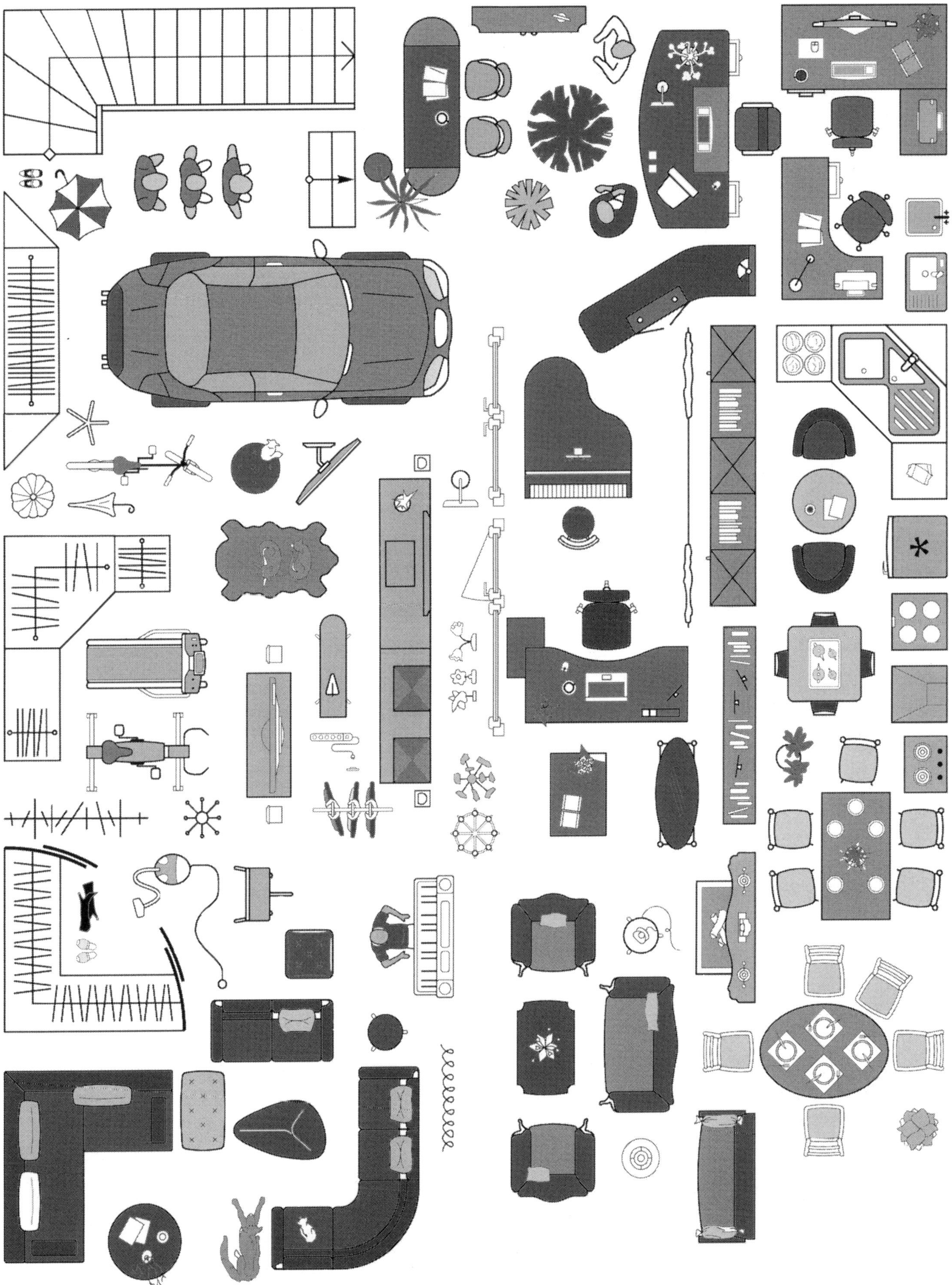

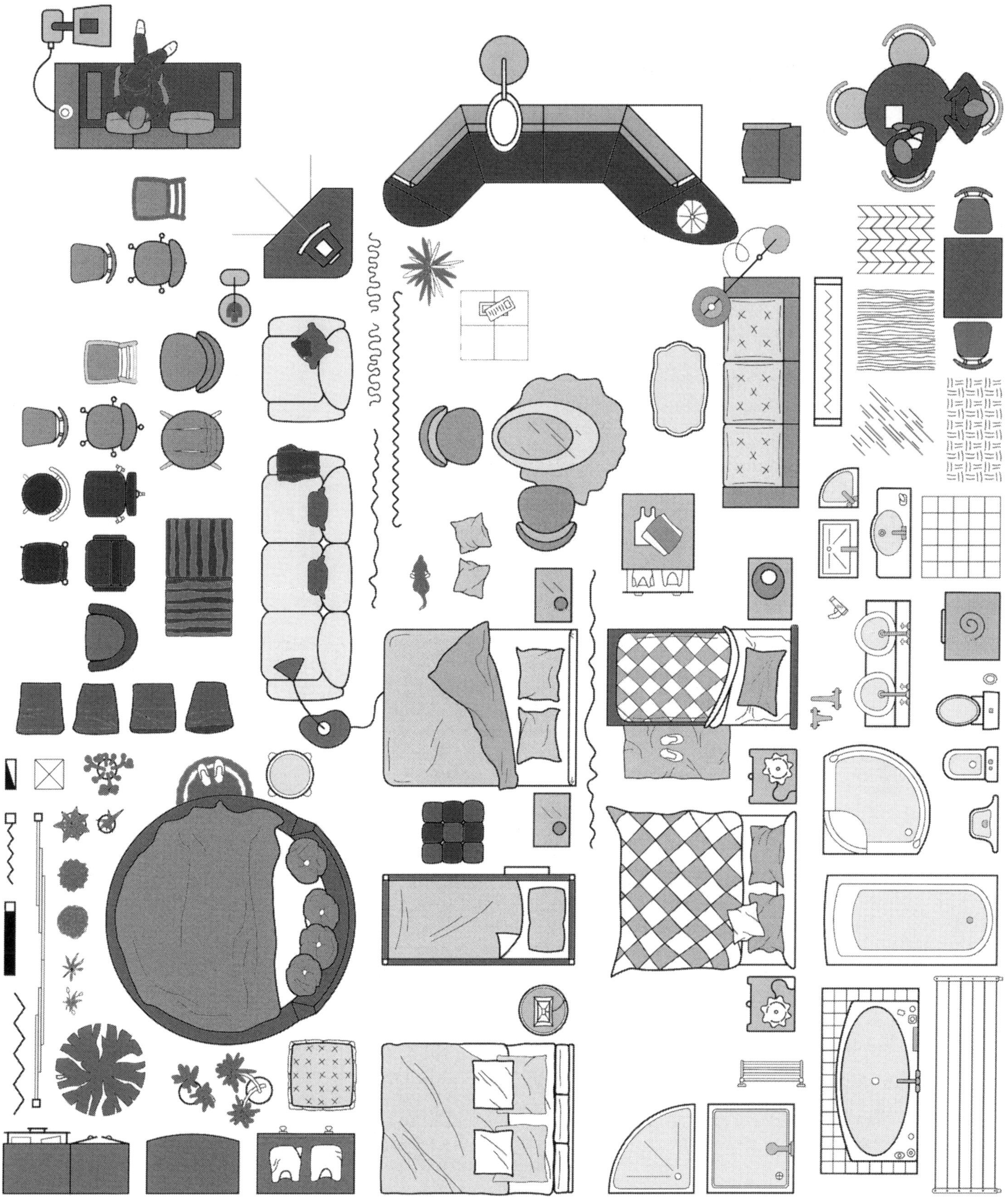

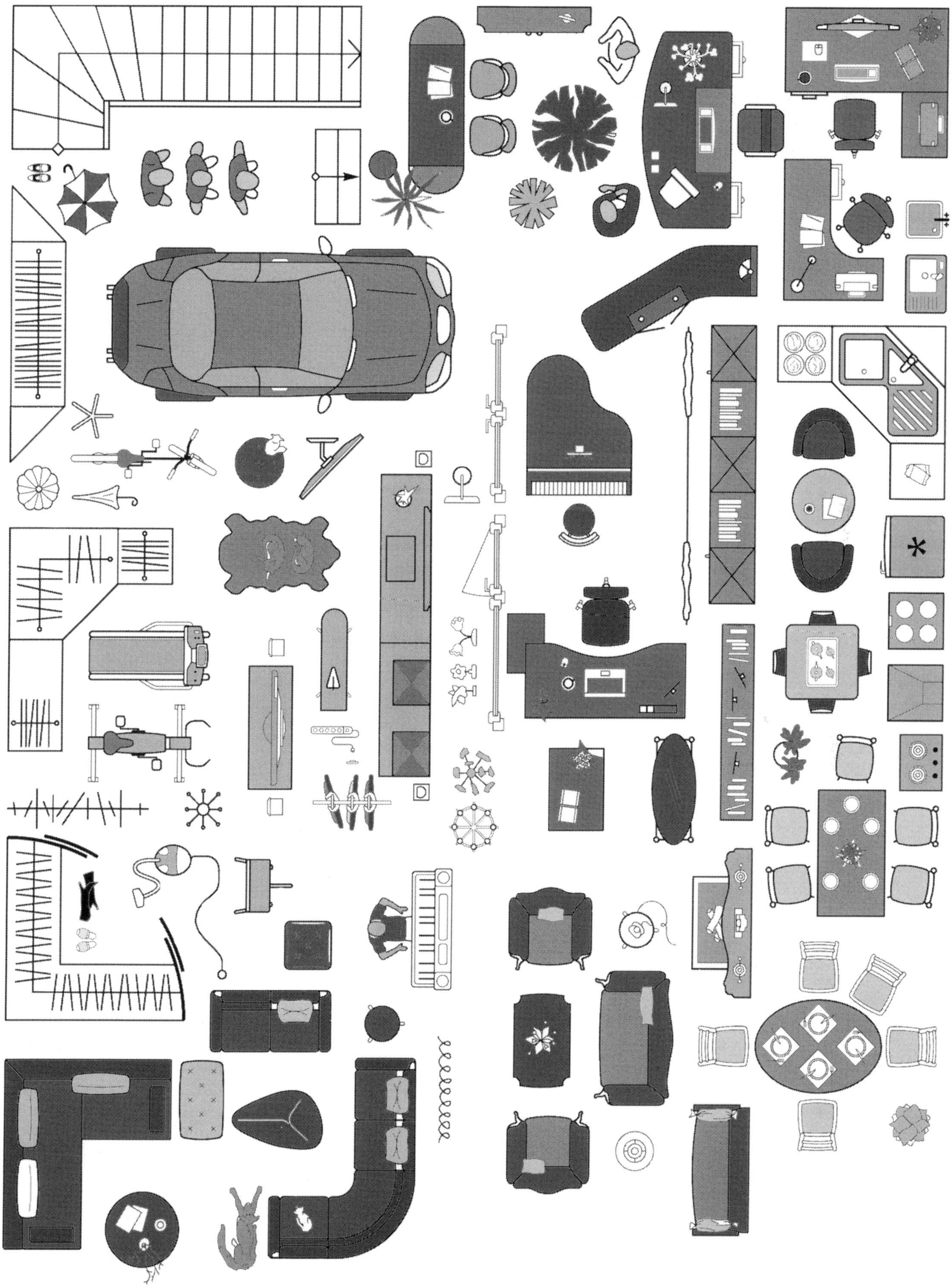

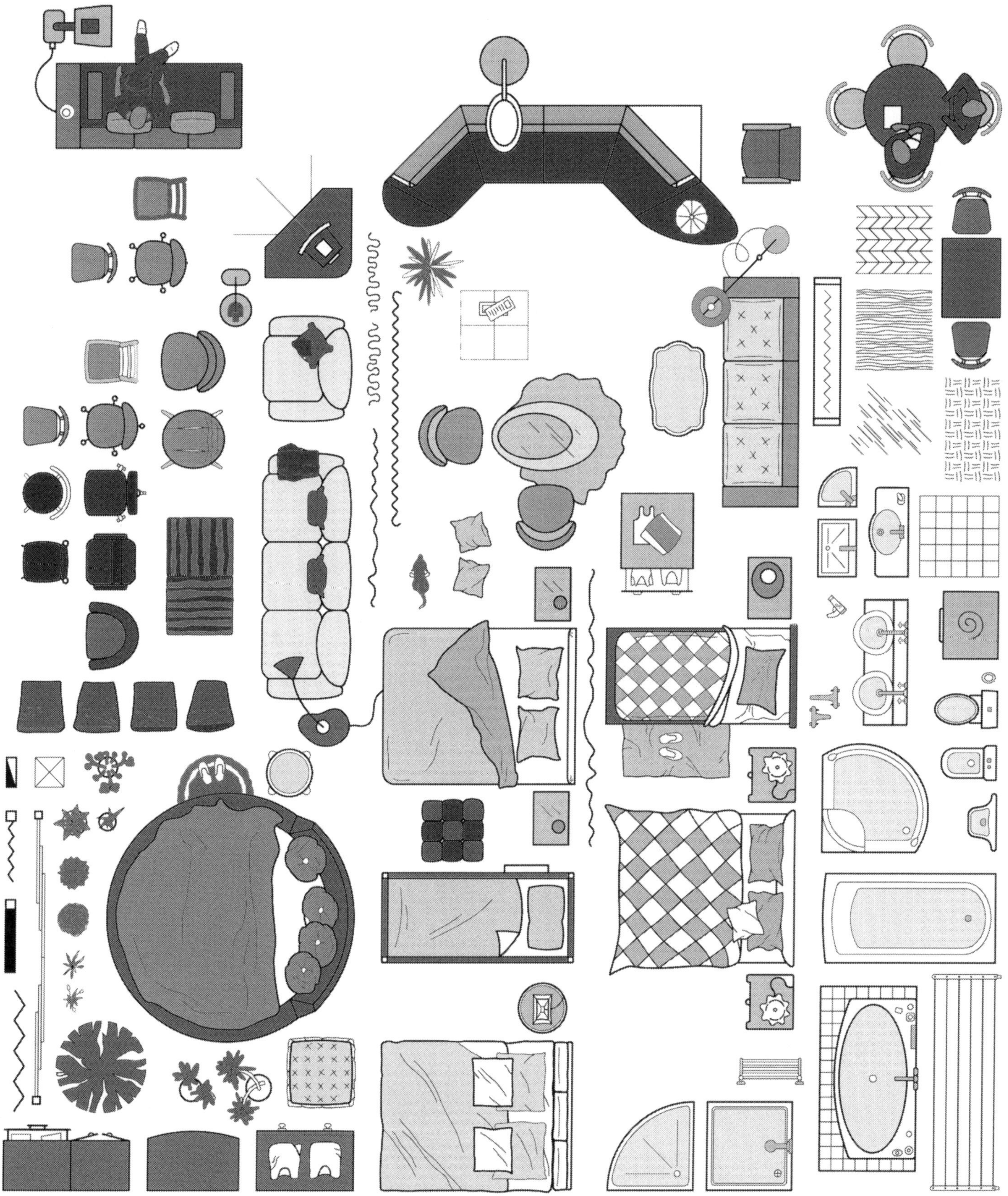

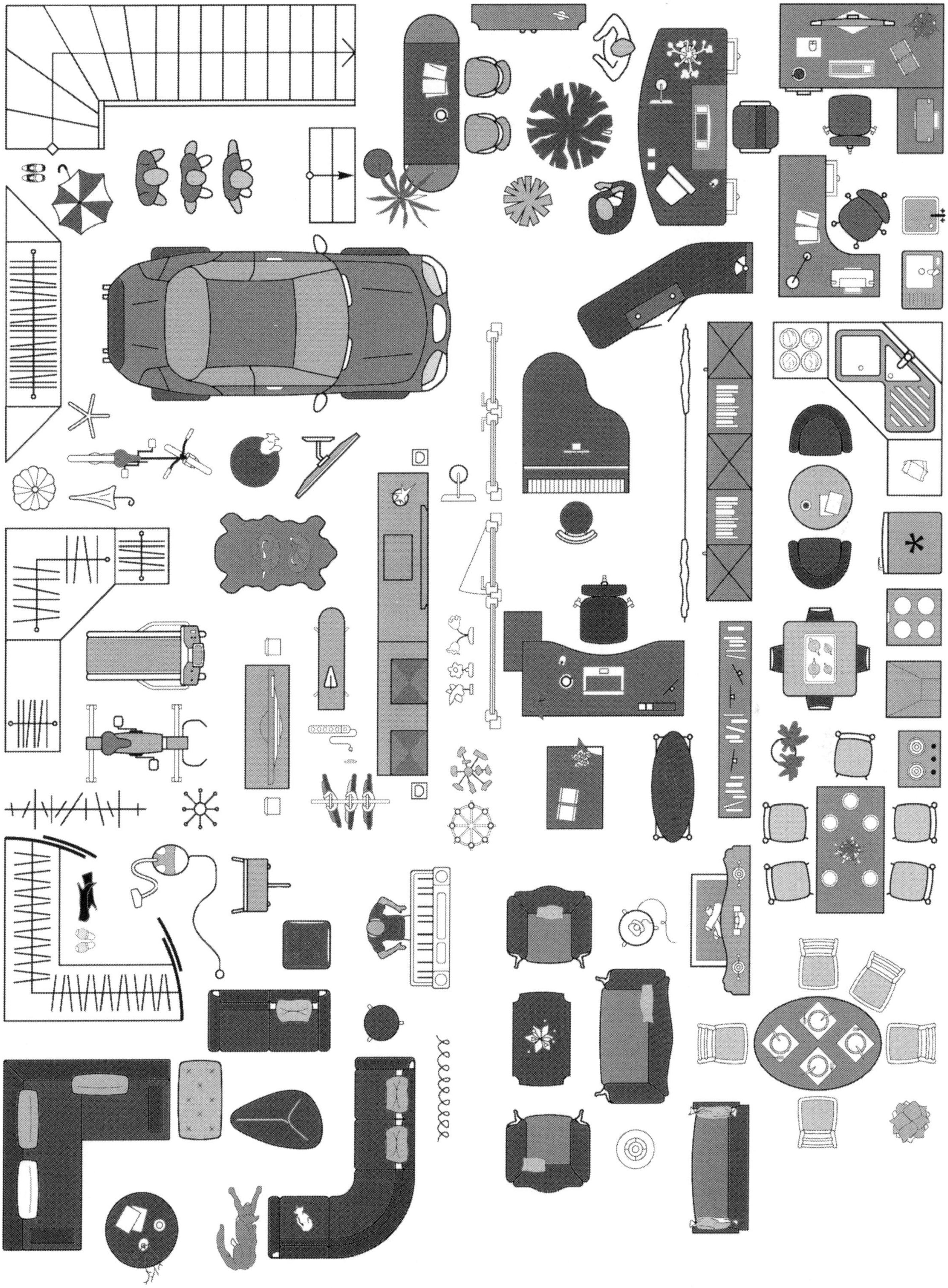

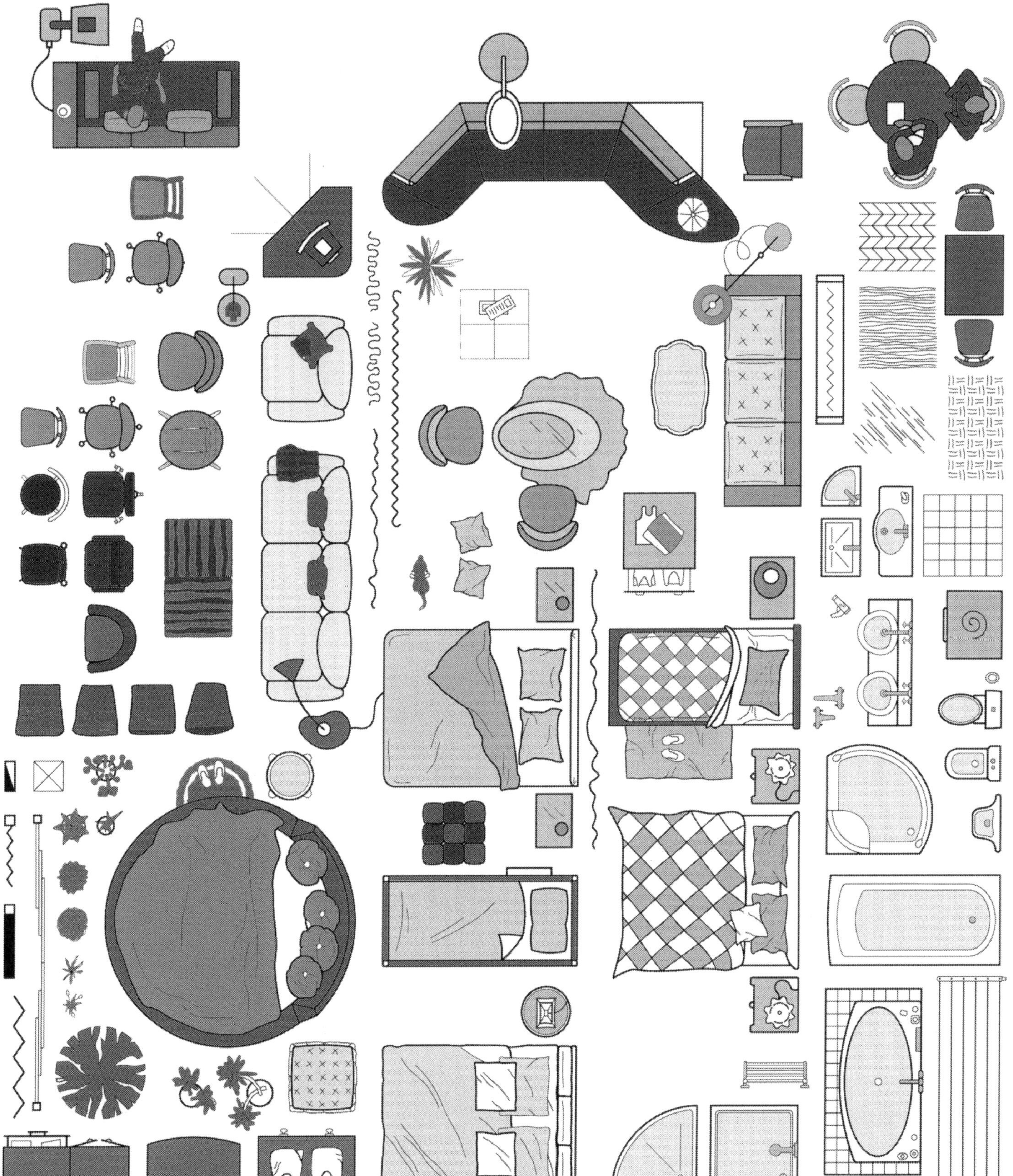

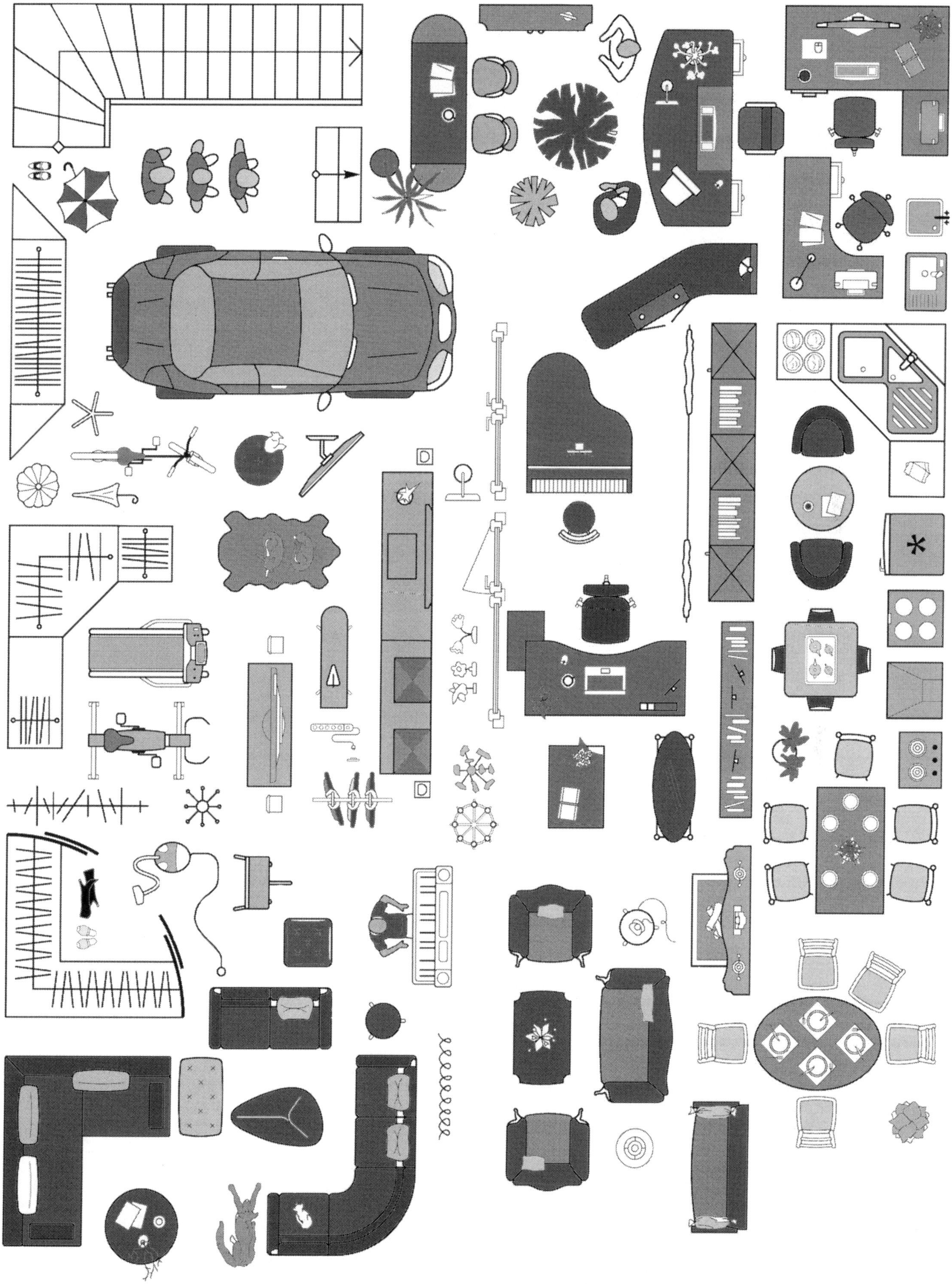

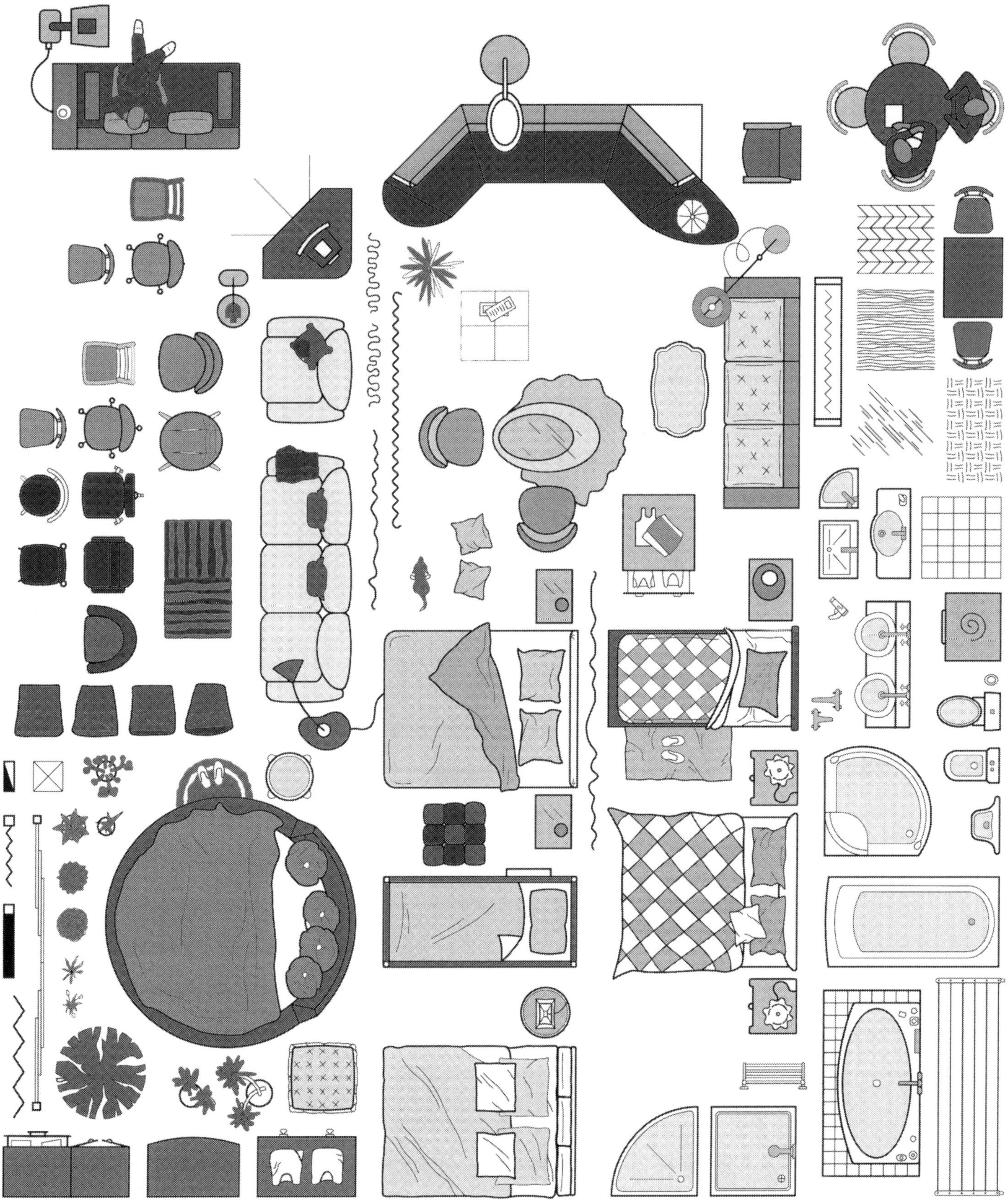

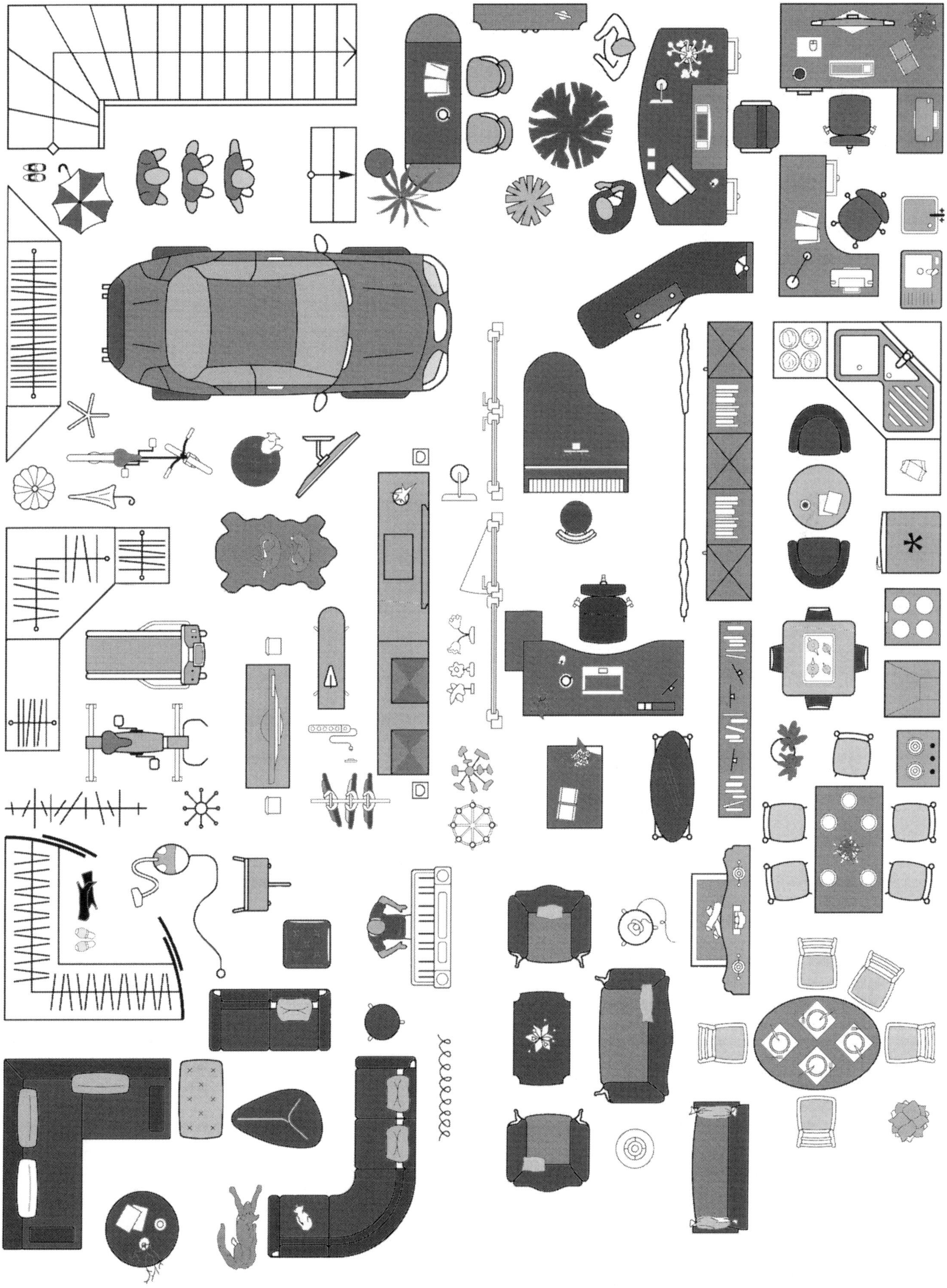

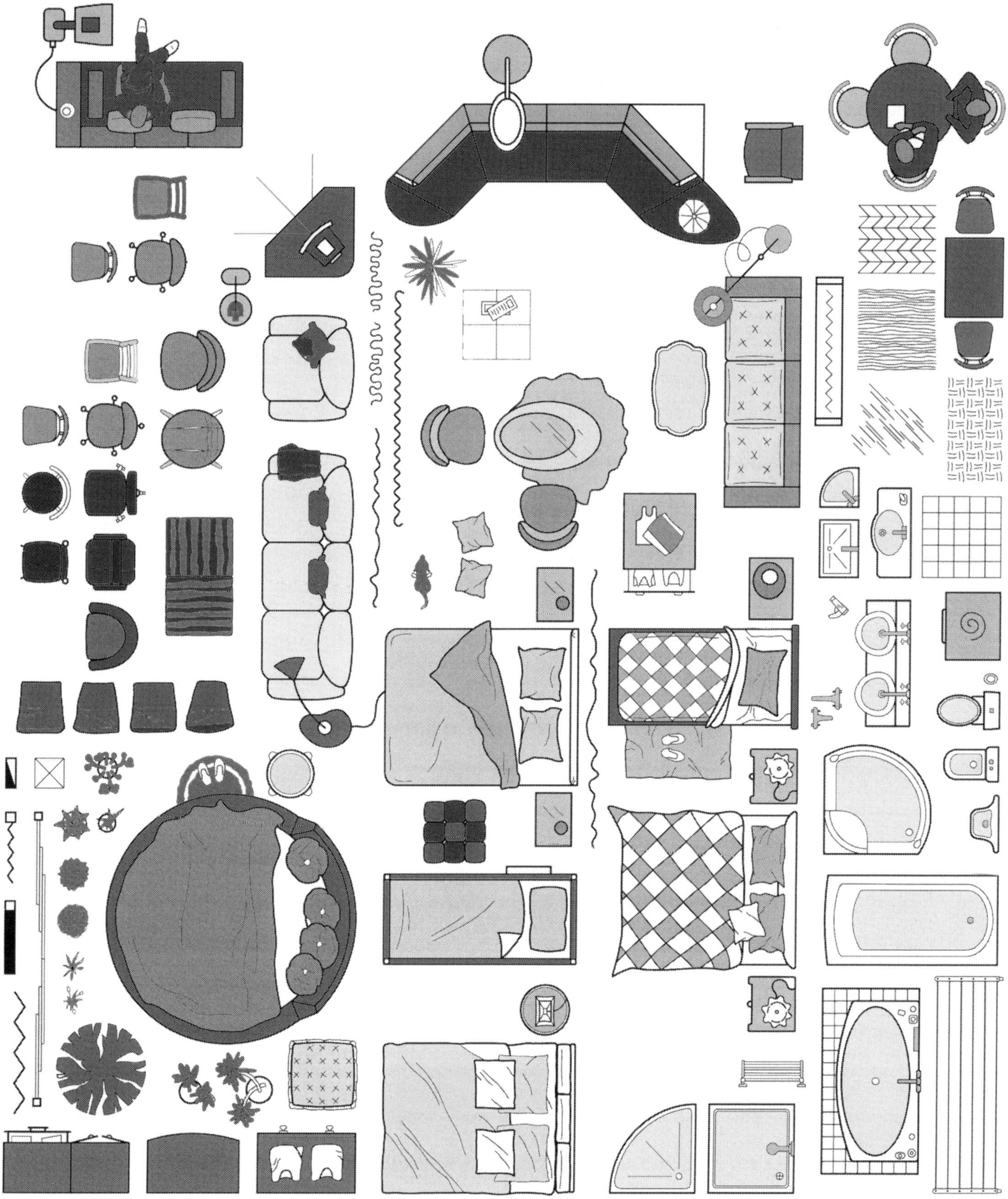

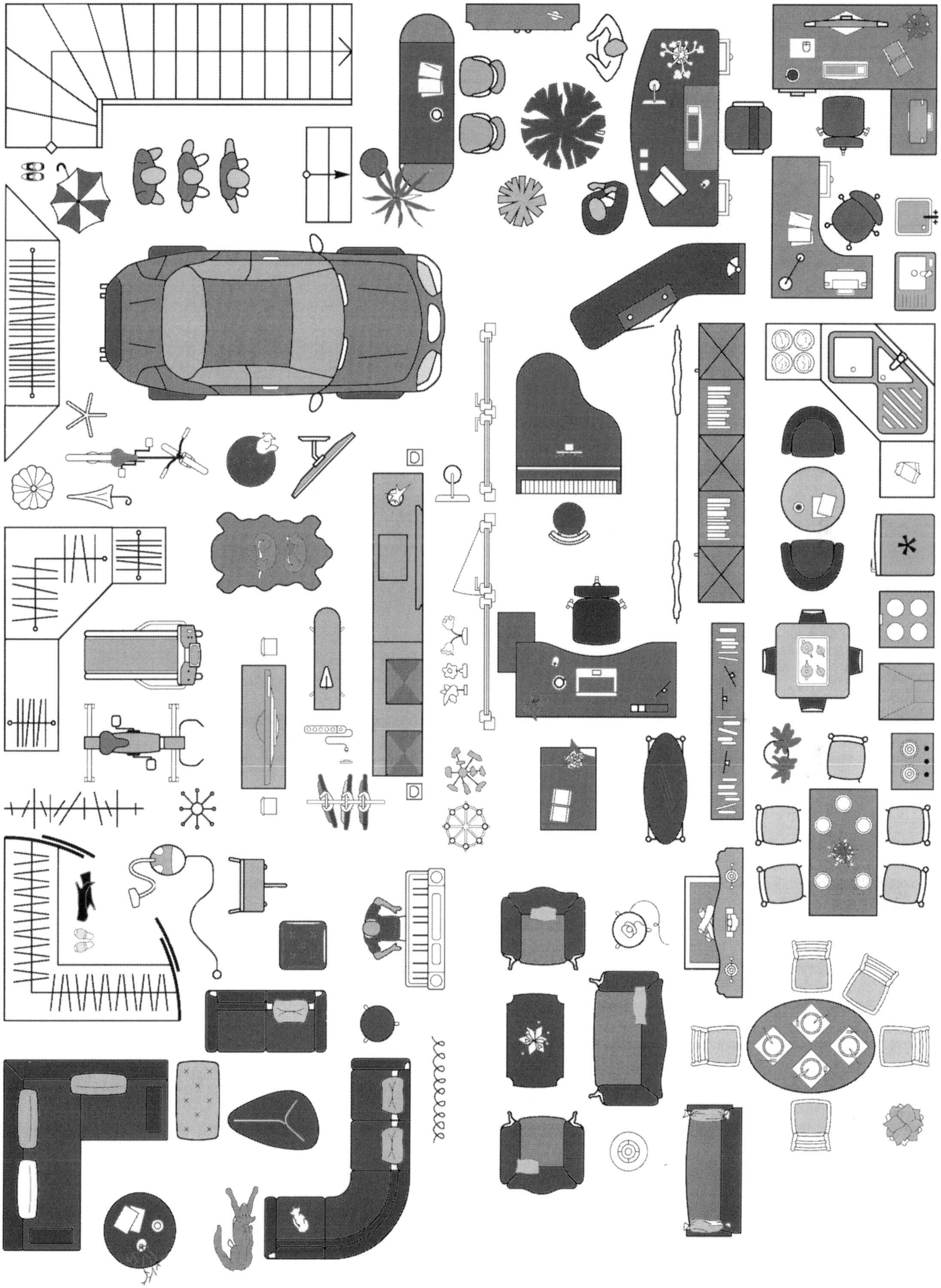

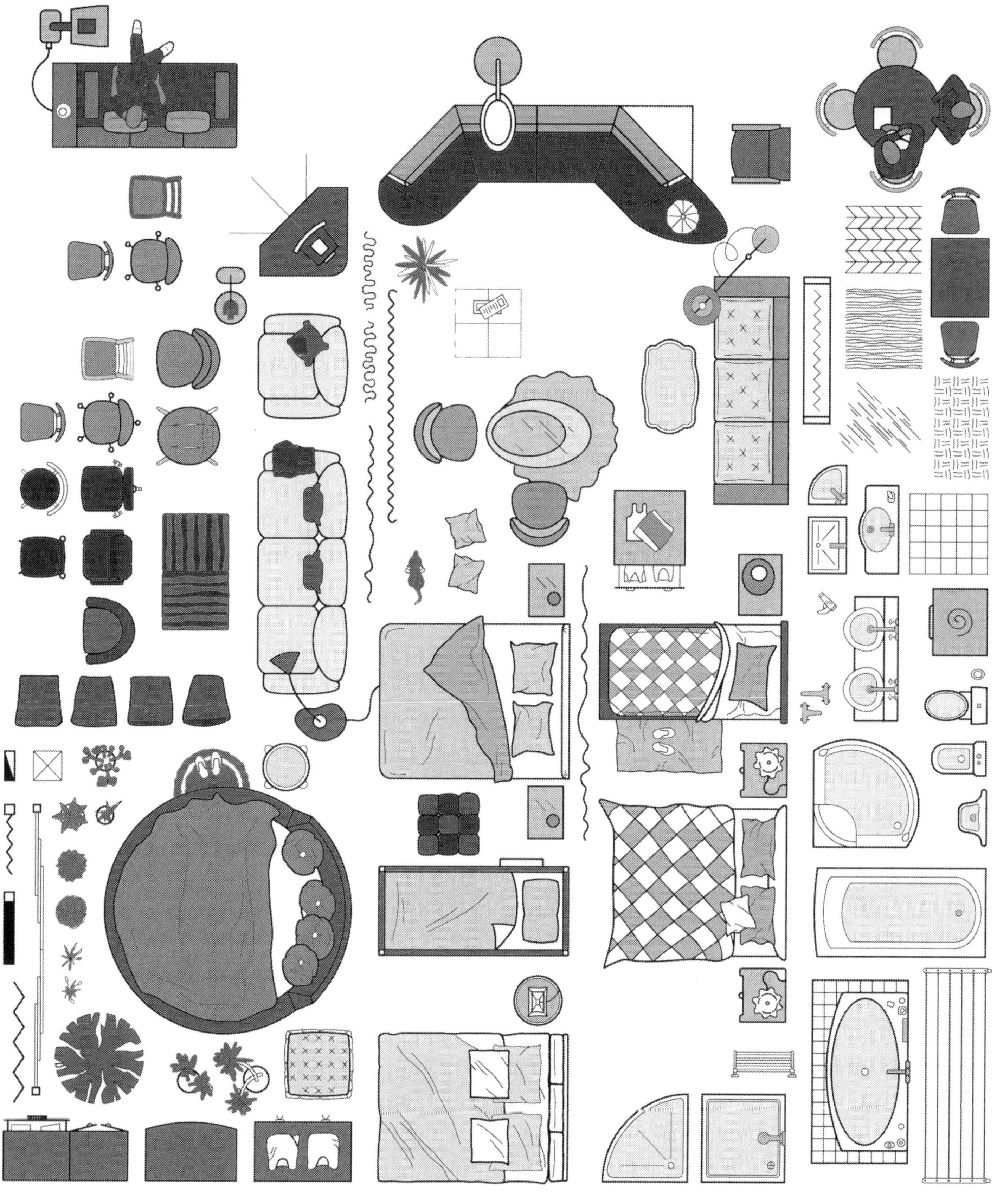